The Kothari Method

— *Book 1* —

Transforming Good People
into Great Leaders

*Three Crystal Clear Steps to
Mastering Leadership*

AMIT KOTHARI

Copyright © 2020, by Amit Kothari
www.KothariLeadership.com
Printed in the United States of America

ALL RIGHTS RESERVED.

No part of this publication may be reproduced, stored in a retrieval system, or transmitted in any form or by any means, electronic, mechanical, photocopying, recording, or otherwise without the prior written permission of the publisher or author. The exception would be in the case of brief quotations embodied in critical articles or reviews and pages where permission is specifically granted by the publisher or author

Published 2020, by Brand Elevate

ISBN: 978-1-952310-95-9

THANK YOU

My deepest thanks to my wife for all of her support and making our lives something I want to get home to every day. And, to my amazing (all parents say that, but I mean it!) children for making me strive to be a better person every day. They don't give hugs much any more, but I sneak my kisses in while they are asleep!

Along the journey, my deepest love and gratitude for Vance Caesar, who is like a father to me. And, the departed Sally Kendrick, who always had open arms for our heartfelt conversations.

I am fortunate to have developed caring family, friends and mentors along the way. The best one comes in the form of an uncle, Uncle Ben…he knows who he is. Aunty Vina keeps us all in check with her loving ways. Friends like Fred and Steve are safe places to share deep thoughts and clean up my thinking. And, thank you to my accountability partners who shape me with hard conversations and deeply held values like Leslie, Jay, Jennie, Kevin, Paul, Susan, Jan, Mike and Justin.

My parents continue to teach me lessons on compassion and servitude. It is a long journey.

Certainly, none of this would be possible without our numerous clients who have the courage to walk the journey of growth and abundance with us. I can only imagine what a pain we must be at times - asking for change this week when we accomplished something "never before in the history of…" just last week… We, at KLE, honor you. We honor you so much that we are here on that path with you, pushing you when you think you have nothing more to give, and collaborating with you when there is no one else to share with.

The insider KLE team members of Michael, Megan, Julie, Craig, Leila, and Carol are so focused on providing great value with a heart of service making them special individuals and a great team. Our professional colleagues like Andy, Mike, Angela and Robin make collaborating at an intense level feel fun.

One final note. I found a new provocateur along the journey last year. Alan Weiss. We have never met in person (yet), but I am grateful to him for not listening to my explanations (excuses) and pushing me to be more impactful.

Thank you.

FOREWORD BY ALAN WEISS

Thomas Malthus, the great English expert on demography and macroeconomics wrote in the early 19th Century that societies could never reach "utopian" levels because advances, such as better food preparation, led to population growth that would be unsustainable. Improvements led to inevitable growth which would eventually be detrimental because of corruption, vice, and misery.

Today, we are focused on sustainability of resources, concerned about the viability of the planet to support not just larger populations (less than 10% of habitable land on earth is occupied by humans) but also provide for a decent quality of life for all inhabitants.

Thus, we are engaged in measures to cleanse the oceans, clean the air, and eliminate pollution and waste. This is a global concern and an important one.

My colleague Amit Kothari has taken that view to an individual level, and asks herein how you and I can sustain our own improvements and positive change. Maslow's famous "hierarchy of needs" showed a pyramidal progression, from security to self-actualization, but in my 30 year of consulting and coaching for the largest organizations and most successful leaders, I've found that people actually travel up and down that hierarchy situationally.

We're seldom "planted" or "affixed" on any one level.

Amit writes in this book about his method for individual, sustainable improvement, no less important for us than for the planet. This is not your stereotypical "self-help" book, which assumes the reader is somehow "damaged' and needs to be "fixed." Instead, he creates a framework within which already successful people can make decisions which will influence the nature and direction of their lives and careers.

As he notes, smart, successful people are usually "hungry" for change. My observation is that hugely successful people, whether business leaders or entrepreneurs, are hugely curious, trying to understand, decipher, and improve the world around them.

But to improve the world, or even the immediate community, has to begin from within.

Unlike Malthus, we're not pursuing Utopia, but we're also not as pessimistic as he about the limited nature of improving ourselves and society. This is a book to create a helping, vigorous, assertive mindset to improve ourselves so that we can improve others.

I know of no greater calling.

—**Alan Weiss, PhD**, author of *Fearless Leadership*
and over 60 other books in 15 languages

A NOTE FROM AMIT KOTHARI

I am fortunate to be around impactful, passionate, intelligent CEOs every day. It was not always this way. I was a consultant coming out of school. I went on to be a public company CFO and a private company COO and CFO. We grew both companies 3-4X in revenue in 4 years and I had the benefit of learning for myself and teaching my teams how to handle a tremendous amount of information and change. When you operate at this level, as I'm sure anyone knows who's reading this book, there's constantly too much information to process and too little mental bandwidth with which to process it all.

"The world is moving too fast," is what we usually say in reaction, as we try to cope with this problem. But the truth is, ALL leaders have the ability to successfully process information, no matter how much or how fast or how strapped and spread thin. All we need is the right personal **framework** *with which to process it, so that we can then strategize and efficiently run our companies, take care of our health and be the leaders we need to be in our families. All too often, some or all of these areas get out of balance and we are reminded of the pain and regret of a life less than well-lived.*

If you're reading this book, you're probably hungry for a change in your life. For some who come to us, it is a desire for ascendency despite self-imagined shortcomings. For many, it is a desire to move chaos to clarity. My great hope is that you're curious, and willing to do the work. This book is full of detailed suggestions, and if you want to bring about change in the way you lead, it can only happen if you put in the time and effort.

This book is short for a reason. You're busy, as am I. That's why everything in here is digestible, so you can remember the content, digest the philosophy and implement it NOW.

If you are a "hobbyist leader," someone who has read hundreds of books like these and executed merely tens of things suggested within them, please stop reading. This is not meant to be entertainment or light reading. It's for CEOs and leaders who are ready to win.

A friend of mine, Dr. Dan Radeicke, taught me about the Optimal Performance Frontier ("OPF") in his Brain-Based Leadership course, a neuro-scientific approach to leadership. We all have an OPF curve and we are performing on that curve as a function of our feeling of safety, which is directly correlated to the mastery of our minds. This book is meant to give you frameworks and practical tips to help you master your mind— to help get you there and keep you there.

At Kothari Leadership, we emphasize EQ+Execution^{TM}. This means we believe sustainable change is achievable only with the right amount of BOTH **emotional intelligence ("EQ") and execution skill**. Without EQ, we hit objections and barriers within ourselves and with others (which we call friction), and when this happens, we give up, disengage, or cause others to do the same. If, on the other hand, we are fortunate enough to have developed our EQ, we may have the emotional strength to process complex demands, but we may still lack the operational skills needed to execute on our growth initiatives or handle those demands. That's where **execution skill** comes into play. That's why, when we have both EQ and execution skill, we can scale growth in any sized organization.

In my 20s, I found myself possessing a sufficient amount of technical skills to be the CFO of a public company. However, I struggled with self-esteem, and was anxious many hours of the day. I'd anxiously await my next investment analyst call from those "smart guys" in New York who could tank our stock with one analyst report (but never would). My anxiety created a constant flow of doomsday scenarios of failure and destruction. This was self-sabotaging, and I am aware now that all those minutes I spent worrying could have been spent leading the team to greater success or learning how to make the company better. I could have been doing—executing— rather than being distracted by my fears and losing control of my thoughts. I've learned a lot since, and now know that what I lacked early in my career was that balance of EQ and execution skill needed to help create sustainable growth in both my company and myself. The blessing was that I did have the requisite amount of execution skill. Not everyone does…and that is where looking for the root cause of a lack of results becomes confusing. Is my problem a lack of knowledge or skills, or how I conduct myself? If I have been a successful founder and/or CEO, why now am I not getting the results I want and expect from myself?

This book is meant to give CEOs and leaders such as yourself the right mindset with which to process information, and to arm you with the exact tools that I use to challenge my CEO clients to help them grow every day.

Please enjoy this practical guide.

Table of Contents

Thank you 3

Foreword by Alan Weiss 5

A Note From Amit Kothari 7

Preface 13

Chapter 1: Have a Framework 17

Chapter 2: Be A King/Queen Maker 51

Chapter 3: Manage Your Energy Right 67

Chapter 4: Conclusion 79

Conclusion 82

Preface

It is important to understand how this book is organized and is to be used, so that it does not become just another book on your shelf.

This book is organized to give you ways to leverage three critical laws of growth that I mastered by working with so many CEOs and leaders. There are also practical worksheets to grind you through the deep thinking needed to solve problems related to each maxim.

This book serves as the precursor to a series of books on the Kothari Leadership 9Lens Framework™, which will teach you all the tactical techniques you need to solve multi-dimensional business problems. Each book will take your practice further, increasing in difficulty as you master different facets of your unique approach to leadership.

Success at your level is about results, not just "good effort." If we are successful, you will keep this book on your shelf and refer to it year after year, awakening to the deeper wisdom in it as you ascend in your self-awareness and business mastery.

Each chapter is organized with a section on:

- » **The subject of the chapter**
- » **EQ Context:** *self-awareness of your own and others' emotions in executing actions in the workplace*
- » **Execution Context:** *business mastery and related practical steps to take in the workplace*

It probably helps to have some context of EQ before reading the book. The godfather of modern EQ, Daniel Goleman, provides his framework:

The Five Components of Emotional Intelligence

1. **Self-awareness.** The ability to recognize and understand personal moods, emotions and motivations, as well as their effect on others. Hallmarks of self-awareness include self-confidence, realistic self-assessment, and a self-deprecating sense of humor. Self-awareness depends on one's ability to monitor one's own emotional state and to correctly identify and name one's emotions.

2. **Self-regulation.** The ability to control or redirect disruptive impulses and moods. The propensity to suspend judgment, and to think before acting.

3. **Internal motivation.** A passion to work for internal reasons that go beyond money and status (both external rewards), such as for joy, curiosity in learning, a love of active immersion and strong personal belief as to what matters in life. A habit of pursuing goals with energy and persistence.

4. **Empathy.** The ability to understand the emotions of others. A skill in treating people according to their emotional reactions, not your own. It is important to note that empathy does not necessarily imply compassion. Empathy can be 'used' for compassionate or cruel behavior. Serial killers who marry and kill their partners tend to have great empathic skills!

5. **Social skills.** Proficiency in managing relationships and building networks, and an ability to find common ground and build rapport.

Your first practical step can be to grade yourself on a scale of 1 (void of skill) to 10 (mastery) on the above. Next, ask others around you (people you trust, with enough maturity) to give you reliable grades. What do you notice in the feedback gaps with others? This is a great jumping off point.

Workbook Worksheet: Emotional Intelligence Survey

Rate yourself from 1 - 10 in each of the components below. Then, ask 4 other people to rate you.

	Me	Person 1	Person 2	Person 3	Person 4
Self Awareness					
Self Regulation					
Internal Motivation					
Empathy					
Social Skills					

...fore you dive in to the substance of the book, it's important to understand exactly what this book is for:

I use my 9Lens framework™ with CEO clients to help them annihilate the unproductive chaos in their lives and get the clarity they need to grow their businesses.

If this is what you need, welcome. Let's get to work.

Chapter 1

Have a Framework

Successful CEOs have a <u>framework</u> for processing massive amounts of information

What is a framework, and why have one? A framework, for our purposes, is a set of rules for organizing data. Think about football. If coaches don't run plays, football would just be a bunch of athletes randomly running around a field causing chaos. Once organized by a strategic leader, players are empowered to leverage a playbook and make strategic moves on and off the field. They are able to master their specialty (i.e., their position), and to measure their progress against a standard of expectations. Take that analogy to a grander scale. In society, with no framework for processing information and codifying societal norms, we'd have total anarchy and at best, chaos would rule.

So it goes without saying that in leadership, it's crucial to have a framework for organizing what appears to be millions of data points a day coming at you in your role as CEO. There has to be a process for critically analyzing what's important, what can wait, and what can be ignored. And no, ignoring something isn't "mean" to others. **Prioritizing is the only way you thrive.** Consider the alternative. If you can't distinguish what is important and what isn't, it won't be long before you're overwhelmed. As soon as that happens, you'll start to disengage from your role and your business, which can obviously have dire consequences.

When a new piece of information comes in, after you've decided not to ignore it, you have to ask yourself: is there enough data to take action with what you know? Is this information going to change your strategic direction or way of thinking about something critical on your plate?

We have to make these thinking processes a **habit**.

The 9Lens Framework™

In Kothari Leadership, we have a model for **processing information**. The model is called the 9Lens Framework™, and it's a multi-dimensional framework for dealing with the complexities of our minds, our roles and a world full of information. To *process* means to assess, refine, critically analyze, prioritize, and take action.

You will look at a single step in the framework and say it's not revolutionary, and you'd be right. It's the ability for the framework to empower you to process any piece of data in the context of the 9Lens framework™ (which organizes all of the moving parts of your business that have you feeling frustrated) that will make it a game changer.

Framework Variables

The 9Lens framework™ has nine variables, organized into three broad categories: the organization, the team and the individual. Don't just read below. Really think about the following questions in each area.

Organization

1. **Strategy:** *Is your overall goal for the people in your company clear, inspiring, and possible? Are you able to prioritize and inspire your team to always be working toward your vision?*

2. **Measurement Systems:** *Do you have measurements that serve to motivate your team members to behave in alignment with your vision? Do those measurements tell them when they're off course?*

3. **Culture:** *Is your company culture one that inspires trust and forgiveness (the path to overcoming a challenge and getting back to work)? Culture ultimately decides how your team spends time—is it on drama, or is it spent ideating and executing initiatives? (As we all know, time truly is money.)*

Team

1. **Roles:** *Does your organizational architecture have all the roles defined to drive your vision forward?*

2. **Processes:** *Do your processes define hand-offs of both authority and information to make it possible for your vision to be achieved?*

3. **Communication:** *Does your team communicate effectively and use time productively?*

Individual

1. **Leadership:** *As the leader, are your core beliefs strong enough to establish trust on your team?*

2. **Emotional Intelligence:** *How do you inspire resilience and persistence in yourself and others?*

3. **Technical (Role) Skills:** *How well do you function in your role as it relates to your vision?*

The 9Lens framework™ was built through practical experience. Think of it like a math equation: each variable adds up to enterprise value growth. They are not all equal, of course. Some things contribute to growth more than others or in different ways, and inevitably, one variable will impact another—think coefficients and correlation. You must evaluate you, your people and your company to understand how each variable will play into your unique approach to results going forward. The end result is the implementation of a system that allows you to expend less energy while creating sustainable, compounding growth.

Key: ● = Organization ● = Team ● = Individual

- The Organization
  - Strategy, Measurement Systems & Culture

- The Team
  - Roles, Processes & Communication

- The Individual
  - Leadership, Emotional Intelligence & Technical Skills

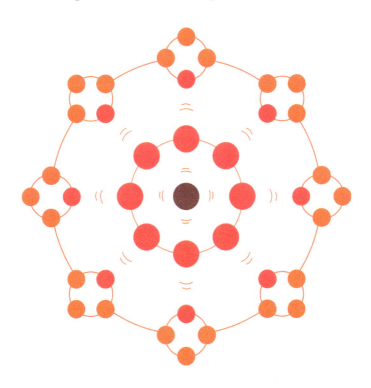

Turning Variables Into Solutions

It is valuable to understand each and every variable, so that you can leverage them to find solutions to challenges big and small. Here are the variables again:

- » Organization: Strategy (includes Vision), Measurement Systems, and Culture
- » Team: Roles, Processes, and Communication
- » Individual: Leadership, Emotional Intelligence, and Technical (Role) Skills

On the **organizational level**, you need a *strategy* that energizes and focuses (how many companies have documented strategies no one knows or cares about?); *measurement systems*, which encourage your team to work towards that strategy and allow your people to know whether they are generally aligned (or not) with the intended outcomes of your strategy; and *culture*, which represents the values of key stakeholders, allows forgiveness for missteps and allows people to rapidly re-collect themselves after mistakes. A culture of *trust* creates more productivity and ultimately less "friction" between the individual, team and organization.

On a **team** level, you need *role clarity* architected by you and other leaders in your organization so everyone knows their part in helping to achieve your strategy (and so you know whether or not you have a full team); *processes* to be able to operate efficiently and keep your team moving towards your vision; and *communication* styles that fit your people and culture. It is amazing to me how much Kothari

Leadership gets involved with healthy communication – it is so necessary and creates such operating leverage. It is more critical than you would imagine. We run into situations where lack of or harshness of communication triggers inefficient behavior all the time. And it goes without saying that when the stakes are high and speed to execution is critical, the risks of disengagement inside a person and amongst people working together are significantly higher when anxiety is higher.

On an **individual** level, you need *leadership skills, emotional intelligence*, and *technical (role) skills.* As we progress in an organization, our incremental improvement in leadership and emotional intelligence is far more powerful than incremental increases in technical skills. How we sustain a growing department in a growing organization requires leadership and emotional intelligence, because we are achieving results through others, not just our own work. Finally, as an executive, we often have quick interactions, leading to less time to make an impression with other leaders and with our team. These quick interactions are fraught with risk. After all, it's wildly easy to derail success by causing friction. For our purposes, technical role skills mean possessing the skills to play your role, i.e., CFO. This does not mean, "As CFO, can you work a spreadsheet?" It actually means, "Can you teach others to use numbers to move the company towards its vision?"

EQ Techniques to Help You Adopt Your Framework

It takes real commitment and a lot of energy to learn and use a framework. This is a long-term approach, and adoption of the 9Lens framework™ takes total engagement. There's a continuum from engagement to disengagement that is valuable to think about here.

Disengagement ←——————— Engagement ———————→

Our goal is to build up the emotional strength required to remain engaged, and when we find ourselves disengaged, to have clear steps that allow us to be aware of and to subsequently stop our disengagement. Fatigue is one aspect of disengagement which is real that can be too easily confused by hard chargers as feelings of "Am I lazy?" Finally, once we're ready to fully engage again, to have the right steps to get us right back to where we need to be.

ENGAGEMENT

Before we worry about your personal engagement, let's set the stage. Culture in an organization should be set to create psychological safety, per the model of my friend Dr. Dan Radeicke. His philosophy is: where people are freed up to be truly happy, psychologically safe and hence engaged, this then allows them to know what true engagement feels like, thus having a frame of reference for when they're not engaged. In unsafe teams and environments, you're almost always going to disengage due to the impact of stress on focus and cognition, so it can be your norm.

Given that context, to be personally engaged, you need to:

1. Deeply believe your personal mission

2. Accurately know your personal motivators

3. Reflect daily on your level of engagement (and measure it)

4. Have your team give daily feedback on your level of engagement

1. Deeply Believe Your Personal Mission

I am sad for those who have not found their calling. For me, knowing my personal mission gives me complete energy, as if from a secret stash of *auxiliary battery power*—especially when things get tough. When I face a challenge and just want to stop, my personal mission allows me to keep going, sometimes even to surpass my prior limits of coping or performing. How did Mahatma Gandhi sustain his fight against all odds for years? Why did Elon Musk sleep on his factory floor? Was it a little dose of crazy, or maybe just full of clarity of personal mission?

This is not an overnight success formula. If you are a normal human being, please begin this practice by reflecting and reviewing yourself. Observe yourself in your daily environment, how you behave and what you feel when you try new things. Have others (with some level of self-awareness and wisdom) observe you, then engage them in honest conversations designed <u>not to make you feel good, but to make you better</u>.

I have a client whose personal mission is to make people around the world healthier with affordable products. Every day, he spends hours and hours in joyful, diligent work towards this goal. I can't think of a single time when he ever spoke about his work without a smile on his face. All the long hours, employee issues, partner issues, distribution challenges…all of that always comes with a smile, because he is doing something that sustains him and fulfills his soul. It wasn't always this way, though. Just a few years ago, his honest personal mission was feeding his ego (even if he didn't know it). He wanted to prove to himself that he could make it to the top. After that, his motivation became money, and optimizing his taxes. That was not a real, deeply held belief of his, and therefore, he found no joy in it. No amount of tax efficiency can deliver success or joy. So, after awakening to that truth, he re-connected with his personal mission. Today, his energy is high, and his day-to-day happy. He has his "flow," and it's sustainable, not fleeting.

Steps to take to find your personal mission:

- » **STEP 1:** Gather more information about what is real to you. Outside of your company, what is your personal mission in life?
- » **STEP 2:** What is a memory that comes to you when you are in a peaceful place of reflection (even amidst chaos)? How many times have you pushed away a dream because it was too

scary to believe it was possible, or too scary to think of the steps you would have to take to achieve it?

» **STEP 3:** What is something you do that gives you a feeling you want to feel again? What are you truly inspired to accomplish? What fills your heart with joy?

» **STEP 4:** How do you know "this is true?" How have you tested your personal mission? Under what duress has your personal mission proven to be true (rather than a mere fanciful thought born from lazy thinking or ego)?

2. Accurately Know Your Personal Motivators

The concept of our personal motivators directs us to the actions we can take to re-charge the *auxiliary battery power* I referred to in the last section. When I graduated from school, I was positive my motivator was title. When I got "the title" in my 20's, I was shocked and dismayed to learn that I felt no greater contentment whatsoever. I realized then that I had no idea what my motivator was. All I knew was that it would take time and a focused effort on my part to find it. I set out on a quest to test various actions and feelings to uncover what motivated me. I have to credit my first coach, Vance Caesar, here in Orange County for my enlightenment, and for teaching me the following exercise. I call it red light, green light. The exercise is on page 26.

Worksheet: Know Your Personal Motivators

Finding your personal motivators involves a lot of false positive findings along the journey. You'll need the energy to work until you find your true motivators. This exercise definitively help you to find it.

 STEP 1   Print your calendar weekly for 30 days (extend if you can; or redo this over 6 months)

 STEP 2   Bring it with you wherever you go, along with a green and red pen

 STEP 3   Clearly mark every meeting you have every day on your calendar

 STEP 4   After each meeting, use your red or green pen to react to that meeting (no other variations, be binary)

Key concepts that feed into red and green:

TIME: Mark your calendar for the coming week. Then let a black pen show which meetings were planned and done, which new meetings showed up on your calendar in green and which meetings got cancelled in red.

PEOPLE: Record who was in each meeting, both those that were held and those that got cancelled. Think about the feelings you had, both with meetings that happened and those that did not.

BEHAVIOR: How did you behave in each meeting? How did others behave? Which gave you energy and which sapped your energy?

Now, pay attention to your feeling in each meeting. What about each meeting is (or isn't) making you feel inspired? What are you trying to achieve? Who is there? How is everyone being? What is being achieved, or not? With that awareness, you can start to look inward and find your motivators.

A new client of mine was struggling with the lack of impact he was making in his organization. He was frustrated knowing he could be doing more, and wanted to his people to see him as more inspiring. We engaged in the red and green exercise above. His first reaction was, "This won't tell me anything new." He doubted that it would have any real effect.

Well, 3 weeks later, after doing this religiously, he found things on his plate that should not have been, meetings being cancelled too often by a particular party and meetings with a lack of focus. He also awoke to the fact that he was currently part of the problem. Once self-aware, we taught him to be the solution.

We worked on learning how to run more effective meetings. For example, we moved data gathering and updates to before meetings, and made them an expectation of attendees. We did not allow participation by anyone who was not prepared.

We urged him to have more assertive conversations with those unwilling to take a stand—this, by the way, included himself. We taught him how to disagree and how to solve critical issues. He, in turn, taught his team.

After four weeks, I got a note, which said: "I blocked my time for my top priorities, and wouldn't you know, I got them done, and done with thought. I said "No" to other meeting requests and people just figured out how to solve their simple issues. I got home to my family and was able to be present at home. How about that, Amit?"

Honing in on your personal motivation:

Once you've finished tracking your red and green calendar markings, take the time to answer these questions:

» Did any red meeting eventually become green? If so, what changed?

» Who was invited to your green meetings? Did you ever do anything to change them up or improve them? What types of people were these – what behaviors did they exhibit?

» In your green meetings, did everyone show up on time? Did everyone remain focused on the objective? Were the meetings productively managed?

» Did the meetings lead to actions that moved you closer to your strategy?

When you have finally found what motivates you, the clarity will calm your nerves and set you on a peaceful path of simply solving problems in front of you as they present themselves. No baggage, just proactive action. In times of challenge, nothing helps kick-start a healthy solution like knowing who you are and what you want.

3. Reflect daily on your level of engagement (and measure it)

At Kothari Leadership, we ask our clients to provide a simple numerical measurement of their emotional reactions to things—a score of 1 being disengaged during the day, and a score of 10 being engaged. We then review what reduces their engagement, and what increases it. We address those items. The use of numbers allows you to measure, "how good is good" and "how bad is bad." That way, you can move your energy towards fixing your state (always striving for "10 out of 10") rather than lamenting your state.

4. Have your team give daily feedback on your level of engagement

Again, measurement over time is key. Have a few skilled and trusted advisors (spouses included!) provide a score on your engagement. If you really want to "get this," do it. The insights and conversations alone will create a network of success around you.

Keep in mind that all of the above is meant to find YOUR level of engagement potential...no one else's. Your potential is a function of how much pre-frontal cortex "energy" you have at any given moment. For example, if you're someone who is genetically wired to be easy-going with a very high threshold for stress and a resilient brain, being "present" may mean the ability to ignore irrelevant stimuli in your current environment (i.e., worries about yesterday's argument with a spouse during a team meeting) for 3 solid hours. If, however, you're someone who tends to be slightly anxious by nature, and may have a quick emotional trigger, you may be doing well to be "present" in that meeting for 1 hour. And, for the person in a totally unsafe psychological environment who is constantly worried about being put down and struggles to connect with team members, that person may do well to be "engaged" for 10 minutes, if ever, in a given meeting.

ENGAGEMENT AND OUR NATURAL TENDENCIES

To optimize your behavior as you engage, you must reckon with your personal tendencies and the effect they may have on your business decisions. For example, at one time in my life, I had a deeply held belief that I was at risk of being wrong (in any decision) and the resulting embarrassment would be unbearable. Well, you can imagine what kind of leader I was back then…over-analyzing, doing things myself, not asking others to help, etc. Over time, I noticed this was severely holding me back, and diligently trained myself not to worry about being wrong, but rather to trust in the value of my judgment. Unsurprisingly, leaders now seek out my judgment, and also seek me out to help them with their own.

Acknowledge your personal tendencies

Are you more conservative with money, a value spender, or loose with your decisions around money? It is helpful to know your tendencies (not just financial). As an example, under stress, you may make a business decision based upon your historical patterns rather than using logical business rationale. There are now many tools to identify tendencies such as DISC, MBTI, Strengthsfinder and tools by professionals like Jordan Peterson, and so on. Neuroscience is now adding another set of tools and techniques to not only expose tendencies but also change them!

Eliminate weaknesses of your tendencies

There are 4 steps you can take to eliminate the potential weaknesses of your tendencies:

STEP 1: Be aware of your bias, when it shows up and how strong it pulls you

Always be aware of your biases. Tell your team about them. Choose your team by selecting people with different tendencies than your own. Allow team members the culture to express their "truth." Incorporate that truth into your decision-making process.

Identifying the impact of your tendencies

What variables will be most impactful in the decision you are trying to make?	What do you tend to do personally regarding these variables (i.e., cost)?	What are the positive implications of your tendencies?	What are the negative implications of your tendency?	What are the business implications of this tendency?	What conclusion can you draw from your tendency?
For example, the conscious variables that I use to make decisions are cost, effort, and value derived.	*I tend to value lower cost items over higher cost items in my personal life, and I tend to believe the lower cost item will be "good enough."*	*I tend to save money and avoid extravagance and what feels to me like gluttony.*	*When I buy lower priced items, they degrade faster and I end up buying the higher cost items anyway.*	*As I grow my business, I realize clients want and aspire to spending more money and they feel they get real value from spending more... their interaction with money is different from mine.*	*I hurt my business by choosing to buy cheaper goods that represent my brand poorly.*

STEP 2: Be aware of your Current Roles

» Your actual role as CEO: is it a doer role or are you more a visionary?

» Your other life roles: are you a parent, a son or daughter of living parents, a provider, a Board Member, etc.

» Your investment horizon (on any particular key decision)

» Your risk tolerance

The number of roles you play and the mastery level with which you play each role will impact the EQ you are able to apply to your new framework. This is to say, at any moment, you have a reserve of energy which gets split amongst roles, so manage the energy mindfully. Yes, over time, you can develop more EQ and more reserves of energy.

STEP 3: Know your Present Context

	Disengaged	**Engaged**
Confused	Lost	Learn/Ask
Clear	Re-engage your purpose	Drive to success

The past is the past. It's important to leave it behind and to see your role and your effectiveness (using the 9Lens framework™) in the moment. Let's break the "context" down into a two-by-two matrix.

One axis will measure engagement level. The other axis will measure clarity (on the path to success), or lack thereof. Depending on where you are on the matrix, you can predict your mindset.

STEP 4: Recall your business's Core Purpose.

Always go back to this. What are you accomplishing with your business, and how can your current challenge move your business' core purpose forward?

With all the above steps, the next move is to take action. Then, reassess these four steps to see if, 1) they are true under stress, and 2) your beliefs give you joy in practice (rather than in theory).

Excellent. Now that you have the tools necessary for engaging in a healthy manner that acknowledges and copes with your natural tendencies, let's prepare for inevitable times of disengagement.

DISENGAGEMENT, OUR POWERFUL ENEMY

There are many forms of disengagement worry, frustration, fatigue, failure, etc. When one occurs, say worry, which is a powerful form of disengagement, you feel anxiety and you can't "think straight," you panic. Your mind races. You become overwhelmed. Your thoughts barrel through your brain at warp speed, eating up your energy and leaving your mind in a jumble and your stomach in knots. You might grasp at your psychological toolbox to solve the problem, but self-doubt kicks in. You wonder if you have what it takes, if you know what you're doing. Sound familiar? We've all been there, and we all know how it feels to have our energy being used unproductively.

So, why do successful leaders disengage?

Well, first of all, it's literally impossible to have laser-like focus 24/7, 365. That's why a framework for assessing information at our level is a lifesaver. One of the leading causes of systemic disengagement is being overwhelmed, and one example of this occurs with the "feeling" of too much data. By data, we're talking new challenges, ideas, meetings, speeches, new people, opportunities, and on and on. Another cause of disengagement is a negative interaction. If someone on your team is causing you problems, or one of your clients or products is proving particularly challenging, your brain automatically tries to shut the valve and protect you from that toxic situation. But, as comforting in the moment as it may be to disengage, you must face these interactions head on. **The cost of not dealing with the issue is exponential.**

The root of disengagement is fear. Not necessarily the fear of the work on your plate, but fear of something deeper—something more subconscious. And, the accumulation or "pile up" of (possibly unrelated) fears. Now, only you can get to the bottom of your root fears, but before you do that, let's arm you with tools for dealing with your disengagement.

At times, I take on clients where disengagement is the core issue. A CEO will tell me he is hard at work and "grinding." I then learn that he is "working" mainly on things of comfort (i.e., dealing with emails, pontificating, attempting to be inspiring by talking a lot) rather than being a catalyst. These are all forms and levels of severity of disengagement. They are also blind spots. Other clients give me different excuses for disengagement—ADD, narcissism, OCD (engaging in too much of one thing can be disengaging from other important activities), and so on. It's all real to these leaders, and sometimes, real period. Other times, it's a made-up problem. Real or perceived, perception really is reality, and all are legitimate forms of disengagement that can be assessed and fixed. I have definitely had clients bluntly claim they have ADD or OCD as a way to explain away their disengagement. Then, weeks or months after putting in some hard work, they were able to throw away their false claims (in their cases it was false, but not in every case), and re-engage with their business.

How do you realize you are disengaged? It's actually quite simple. The best thing you can do at all times—is listen.

1. Listen to the results you set out for yourself. *Are you getting what you want?*

2. Listen to your feelings on how your time is being spent. *See calendar exercise covered earlier.*

3. Have your trusted advisory group regularly review some of your data points (what you're dealing with) so they can get to know your "coasting state" and your "high performing state." And obviously, listen to them when they tell you you're disengaging.

A symptom of disengagement is making mountains out of molehills (i.e., subconsciously guiding yourself to disengaged behavior). This tendency is extremely common, and totally unproductive. If you find yourself doing this, check in on the above steps. Listen to yourself and the people you trust, and if needed, refer to the next part of this chapter—*re-engagement*.

The great challenge with being disengaged is that you have to know when it's happening in the moment. You have to be able to be aware in those times. This is most helpful when you are predisposed to being in denial.

How you come back from being disengaged is covered in the re-engagement section below.

If you find yourself not committing to your work or a particular challenge, or generally disengaging, see on page 38.

Worksheet: Engagement Analyzer

Being engaged is one of the most powerful tools you possess. When you're present and engaged, you're operating at your full potential.

Any time you feel disengaged, answer these questions to reclaim your **presence:**
What am I feeling about my current situation?

What's the reality of this situation versus my perception?

What do I have the potential to learn (i.e., change "my reality") if I allow myself to engage with this situation?

What am I trying to solve or achieve?

How can I repurpose this into a productive set of action items to recapture my momentum?

RE-ENGAGEMENT

If you find yourself in a downward spiral of disengagement or worry, STOP. Imagine time STANDING STILL. Just until you catch your breath. Take a deep one, then another. And now, use this method to regain control:

STEP 1: Do something that satisfies your personal mission

When I'm feeling disengaged, I reach out to someone in need. No matter what's going on, helping someone helps me "switch on" like a light bulb. It's my fountain of youth, my absolute source of energy that is 100% successful and available to me, all the time. As a matter of habit now, when I am not feeling 100% committed to something, I find a person in need, and start a conversation. When I begin to help and coach this person, it takes no energy and, in fact, creates energy in me. This is my personal solution.

For my personal friend, it is the concept of stepping away. Go for a ride, take the day off, get away from the desk.

What's yours?

STEP 2: Make (or review) your Gratitude List

Five at most should do the trick. This gives us a framework for making the most out of our triumphs, including overcoming disengaging moments.

STEP 3: Identify the root cause of your fear, and take an action to solve it

In order to overcome individual challenges, we must honestly face our deepest fears, not only the ones we are aware of, what lies beneath. By design, our deeper fears are hidden in our blind spot because we are afraid to address the actions required to fix them. Only active engagement on the fear will solve them. The fears below the known fears are the hardest of all to process, but the most important to our future scalable success. Facing these fears means gaining true control over your energy and your emotions, leading to your ability to conquer every challenge, no matter how great.

I ask my clients to inventory their beliefs regularly. Your thoughts are often combined and intertwined between others like roots of a tree. When you are able to untangle them and to see the individual thoughts, then you inventory the thoughts into three categories:

Core Beliefs

- Core beliefs are defined as thoughts which serve both you AND your stakeholders. An example is, "When I speak my truth with humility and lay the foundation for feedback, I am not afraid to share big feedback."

Fear-laden thoughts

- Fears are thoughts that don't serve BOTH of those conditions. An example is, "I am an imposter, I can't speak up now."

Gaps in experience

- A thought that is a gap in experience ("I don't know…") is simply an indication you have to gain the necessary knowledge. An example is, "I don't know how to raise $10 million."

When you inventory the thoughts, then:

» Step 1: Keep the core beliefs

» Step 2: Kill the fears

» Step 3: And learn through the gaps in experience.

You will find that you will gain more and more momentum as you kill the fears and solve the experience gaps. Then, overcoming your fears requires some deeper dive.

When you break down individual situations, be aware how severe the situation is. You will have the same beliefs and fears whether at home or at work. The more intense the situation, the more you will need someone else to be present during the situation and giving you independent feedback on your words and actions. The goal is to make the subconscious *conscious*.

As an example, I have a client who has spent his lifetime protecting himself. He is very good technically at his job, and will put in the time to get the work done. Due to this effort, he has been promoted. Now, as one of the leaders of the company, his behavior is not matching the level of his role. He's refusing to participate in company-wide initiatives claiming he's too busy (not a fact, and regardless, a deal killer on living up to his responsibility) and appearing disengaged in group meetings.

My first attempt at coaching was not to point out the solitude in which he was operating. We muddled through some complex business situations and we had to discuss the separation of tactical challenges from emotional blockages. I had to point out the root cause of a problem wasn't other people and his perception of their bad intentions, but what he could control – his knowledge and his approach. When he feared the reaction of others (not engaging, not agreeing with him, yelling at him), he did not even choose to play. As such, he never developed enough skill or emotional resilience to win in these situations (which, when taken to an extreme, causes cultural poison in a company and lethargy in execution, thereby killing scalable growth!).

Slowly, my client came to understand that he had more influence and power over what happened and is now participating more actively and showing his enthusiasm. The root cause in this situation was not effort or anyone else; it was his ability to wrestle with his overboard protection mechanism, a voice in his head that kept warning him to be careful. That voice then created interpretations of other people and their intentions as bad – remaking any real example into a horror flick of bad intentions for my client.

When I showed him his overwrought imagination, only then could he allow his kind heart, passion to please, and drive to shine. And, at that point, others saw it too. Now, he is joyfully participating and engaging in leadership of the company. When you're feeling motivated enough to overcome your fears, you will take action. When you do…

- » Start acting toward your vision – each action is moving you closer to your vision or away from it, and know that there is no "neutral"
- » Be aware of your thoughts and purpose
- » Explore and reassess conflicting desires or fears
- » If you act differently than your words, then you know you have not identified all of your fears.
- » Become a student of people

Not only have I noticed this process happening with those whom I've coach. It's happened to me, too. When I took on public speaking as a personal goal, I was excited and eager to step up to the plate. But then I was asked to speak at a conference, and immediately my stomach churned and my heart went into overdrive as my mind yelled at me: "What the hell did you just commit to?!"

On the journey of public speaking, I encountered various stories I told myself. I had to make my subconscious *conscious*: in the end, I could speak and I could stand in front of people – that was reality. My job was to identify the fears that popped up – like monsters in a video game – not real, but scary nonetheless, as they devour life points.

In the beginning, I wouldn't let anyone know that I desired speaking opportunities. As you can imagine I wasn't getting speaking assignments and told myself there aren't many to get so I'd be lucky to get just one.

But at one meeting, I liked the person so much (and therefore felt very safe) that I felt comfortable asking if there was an opportunity to speak. The reply was immediately: "Yes! Of course!"

Subsequently, I now ask and intertwine my request consciously into a conversation, and I either get a "yes" or "No, I don't, but I know of an organization that…" Magic!

My other insecurity was deeper: I'd find that during the practice of my speeches, I'd prepare the PowerPoint a month in advance, and in a flurry of excitement, I'd hem and haw around practicing the text of the speech. I found that I loved the technical part of the work so I hurriedly developed slides for the speech, but I was afraid of the speaking part. I made up stories that I had writers block. I also didn't practice as I planned. Then, a few days before the speech, I'd start getting anxious and cram like it was finals week and I hadn't attended a class in weeks.

The big day would come, and I'd give the speech, it would go well (not great, though), and I'd look back and reflect that I didn't enjoy the whole lead-up to the speech, and be mad at myself knowing that I could have done better. So I ruminated and found that my fear of being judged was stopping me. The complex part was something that is probably quite common and yet is hard to discern: *if I don't practice, I could always blame it on the lack of practice if I bombed!*

I wasn't in a positive mindset – I was in a defensive mindset. From there, I decided my vision was to enjoy speaking and touching more lives.

Now I remind myself of that vision when I am feeling anxious. I'm now preparing for speeches with a feeling of humble servitude and sharing, which centers me – I now see the value in preparing, during which time I create new coaching content or a way of communicating an idea. *And* speech preparation coaching is added to my business, too! Who knew that from anxiety could come creation?

That was three years ago, and I'm happy to report that I enjoy public speaking so much that it feels more like a hobby or a treat, and I've gotten a great deal of business from my speaking engagements too.

COMMITTING TO YOUR FRAMEWORK

Now that you are engaged and have the steps to both fight disengagement and to re-engage, it's time to implement a program that reinforces your commitment to your new framework for processing complex levels of information.

1. **Be aware of losing commitment**. *If you keep a daily log or diary, you can note a line item to remind yourself to use your framework to remain engaged in your work and committed to your vision. You can also keep a visual of the steps of your*

framework on or near your desk. In the best of cases, you can teach your team your framework so it becomes part of your team's language and culture.

2. **Remind yourself to behave with intention.** *It's easiest to set a specific time daily for this reminder. You can even set an alarm.*

3. **Make a habit of catching yourself whenever you forget your framework.** *The uses for a framework in daily life as a CEO abound. There should be more than enough to work on and process daily, so the lack of use of a framework should be an unusual circumstance.*

4. **Put your framework in your weekly team meeting agenda.** *This one speaks for itself.*

"In working with frameworks now, instead of thinking about individual transactions, from daily interactions with my people to requests from clients to market data to specific software functionality, I now realize using a framework puts the many individual pieces of data into a systematic structure that allows me to make decisions faster and be more assured that those decisions align with where I am taking the company. Without such a framework, there is a risk that I will become too micro-focused and make a rash decision that will be out of alignment, and thereby confuse my employees, customers or stakeholders."

- **Jay Gundotra**, *CEO, eNow Inc.*

Execution Techniques to Maximize the Impact of Your Framework

There are a couple of things worth noting about the Kothari Leadership 9Lens framework™. Knowing these things will help you make the most out this methodology for processing information and facing challenges.

Know that this framework plays well with others.
Great news about this model is that you can easily combine it with other tools you use already. For example, if you like Scaling Up by Verne Harnisch, most of his model fits in the Strategy variable. If you are a Daniel Goleman fan, most of his work falls into the Emotional Intelligence variable. There is a wealth of wisdom from amazing thinkers and authors, and it's okay to use and love other models.

Call Upon Your Top 3 "Personal Board of Advisors."
Success doesn't happen in a vacuum. Even leaders need advisors.

Here are guidelines for choosing your top 3:

1. You must come to an agreement with them that they will always tell you the truth, and always be willing to challenge you. Your faith in this process will depend on radical honesty.

2. They must be able to brainstorm problems small and large, broad, vague, specific and otherwise. Intellectual flexibility is key.

3. They must not judge. Only in a safe environment can you problem-solve and re-engage.

Use *system thinking*.

If you are a *transactional* thinker, you think, "What would solve this problem I have?" and come up with a singular solution, such as "Joe can take care of that!" or "We just need one more service agent to handle the workflow." In *systems* thinking, you look at the 9Lens framework™ model and ask yourself questions like, "Under my current strategy, I have X volume now, but I want our volume to be Y in 2 years. Through what mix of personnel, training, role clarity and process automation will I solve this volume issue?" This multi-dimensional thinking is difficult—especially in times of stress—but it is essential to solving complex problems. Anxiety is completely normal, but it's not an excuse for simplifying a problem. It's important not to use *transactional* thinking as a crutch because it's easier and we're too frazzled to play multi-dimensional chess.

Chapter 2

Be A King/Queen Maker

Successful CEOs have the courage to have hard conversations. Master this skill, and become a King/Queen Maker.

CEOs come in all shapes and sizes, and they all possess a huge range of skills, personalities and communication styles.

You get hired as a CEO, and the automatic assumption is, you're a pro at having hard conversations, right? WRONG. This is one of the most common misconceptions about the job. Sure, some CEOs are born bold. Some are even born brash, harsh and even cruel. But are those CEOs effective? Perhaps at times, but for the most part, probably not. What I teach to all of my CEO clients, and what I want to impart to you, is that the best CEOs are KING/QUEEN MAKERS. This means they not only master their potential, but they *encourage, empower and embolden everyone around them to be their best.*

Now, nature doesn't simply create King/Queen Makers who perform at this level without coaching. We all need people in our corner to show us our blinds spots and to educate us to be better. And what does it take someone in our corner to show us our blind spots? You guessed it: the ability to have hard conversations. They're everywhere—and sometimes we're on the giving end, sometimes the receiving. Either way, CEOs **must** master them.

WHAT ARE DIFFERENT KINDS OF HARD CONVERSATIONS?

There are a million, but here are just a few you may encounter:

- Firing an executive that has been with you from "the beginning"
- Calling someone out during a meeting for controlling or overpowering others or eating up time
- Tough financing negotiations
- Complex Mergers and Acquisitions negotiations
- Asking others to take on a greater share of the burden of leading
- Addressing a C-level executive who has some great traits, but is failing miserably in specific ways, and having to put them on a performance plan
- Driving a passive aggressive person to stop creating a culture of blame and fear, and to be more of a team player

Side Note: Of those examples above, for those of you with experience, doesn't the last one seem the most difficult? This is because it's emotionally complex dealing with a negative, passive aggressive person who may otherwise be effective at their job. You may try for a long time to set this person on the right path, but eventually find that it's impossible to change their core personality into something that fits with your team. This will lead to another difficult conversation—replacing that person. But every now and again, you may successfully help one of your more difficult yet productive employees transition into true team players. THIS is an accomplishment, and a rare one at that.

THE BEST WAY TO HAVE HARD CONVERSATIONS

Simple truth: in order to successfully have difficult conversations, you must add two skills to your emotional toolbox: **courage** and **influence**.

Now, notice that I did not say you need to be nice, nor did I say that you need to be honest. What you need to be **effective** is the courage to say the right thing in the moment. A great word a friend gave me for this is "specificity." Ambiguity kills. Say the truth, but at the right time so that your counterparty can hear you effectively. You'll know whether or not they heard you based on whether or not they take productive action as a result of your words..Action in the direction of your vision is evidence you were **effective**. Anything else is "less than."

STEP ONE: STOP TRYING TO BE LIKED

Yes, even at the CEO level, we all harbor a secret desire to be "liked." This beckons back to our childhoods, and plagues our every social interaction. But I promise you, the sooner you master getting over this pointless, never-ending goal, the quicker you'll learn to be an effective leader who can have hard conversations. Imagine if you stopped worrying about idle chitchat? What would your team think of you? The answer is simple. They'd come to know you as someone who means what he/she says, and they'd learn to take note. That's influence. If you have the courage to speak when it matters, you'll rapidly find yourself in possession of the precise tools you need to master strategic conversations—no matter how challenging or hard for your colleague(s) to hear.

STEP TWO: OPERATE WITH YOUR TEAM'S BEST INTEREST IN MIND

Coming from a childhood of high verbal tension, I tended to avoid hard conversations. I joked. I kept opinions to myself. I let things fester by staying silent. It is no small feat to find myself decades later at a place where I have not only personally rebounded, but grown into a coach to CEOs. Every day, I give clients my honest and unbridled opinion, no matter how harsh. It's okay, though, because I always do it in a way that honors them and creates a safe space for them to process and act upon these ideas and thoughts. It takes courage to tell people what you think, and that comes from practice, refinement, and the product of this, skill, to say something that will be heard in a manner that is desired. So where does that skill come from? (See below: "EQ Techniques") CEOs aren't the kids in the back of the class with their hand down. They're up front with their hands raised, and if you're not that kid now, you will be once you have the right framework for processing information and executing upon it.

When you're at a point when you can successfully have hard conversations, get ready to make your teammates yell or cry or even throw something. Many of my CEO sessions lead to red faces and tears. But at their core, these sessions are built upon a foundation of trust, so there is also laughing, reconciliation and positivity at the end of these challenging interactions. My clients understand that my words and ideas are always shared with their best interests in mind.

THAT is how you become an effective leader. Become known as someone who isn't cruel for cruelty's sake, but rather an honest assessor of what is needed and how to get your company to the next level. And, make sure there is something in it for them. Something for them to strive for, to learn, to enjoy, to benefit from, etc.… or they won't be motivated to endure the discomfort of change. Sure, sometimes it may be in the best interest of your team to let someone go. This will surely lead to a hard conversation, or several. But ultimately, if you operate with your team and company's best interests at heart, it really will be okay. And remember, it's not about being liked. You were hired to lead, which isn't always rainbows and water cooler gossip.

EQ Techniques to Help with Hard Conversations

Hard conversations are veritable hotbeds of emotion. Control these conversations by first mastering your EQ context. To do this, you must:

1 Understand your feelings first.

2 Clear your subconscious blockers. Leave your baggage at the door.

3 Remind yourself of the freedom you will feel after having this hard conversation.

4 Understand the emotional state of the person you are addressing. Empathize with his/her potential reaction by placing yourself in their shoes.

5 Be ready to paint a picture of success to the person you are addressing.

1. **Understand your feelings first.**

What are you like? Are you bold or shy, calm or easy to anger? You have to know the answer to this deceptively simple question before engaging in a hard conversation, so you can successfully catch yourself from playing to your emotional stasis rather than acting in a healthy manner. In other words, knowing yourself can help you present a difficult topic without saying or doing something unproductive.

We all have triggers—things that depress us or cause us to be anxious or disengage. When we understand our feelings, we're empowered to clear some of our subconscious blockers. To do this, you need to first understand your deepest motivators. When you know what drives you, these things will fuel your passion and motivate you to have hard conversations at a healthy pace so your business can keep growing.

Whenever I am in a cycle of avoiding or being depressed, I do something to learn (i.e., read) and/or place myself in service (i.e., call someone in need). 100% of the time, my energy rises and I start taking action—even if that means having tough talks with my team. That is how I know those are my motivators – it is proven. We need these deep motivators to work through our fears and our blockers, to overcome our doubts, and to trigger the infinite emotion available to us when our minds are clear.

I have a client who has a growing business with about 50 employees. She has been in business for 15 years. She is a good leader. She also has changes in her temperament that escalate into anger and blame. She's instilled fear in her ranks with her unproductive, Jekyll and

Hyde-like persona, and is just now coming around (with coaching) to admitting that this is a problem. Her behavior has placed an invisible ceiling on her company's ability to grow. Although she flies off the handle, she also is kind, charismatic, and 90% of the time, a fun-loving person. We are working through making her more self-aware, keeping her personal conversations separate from her business conversations, stopping her from talking about "what she is feeling" during the work day and focusing her energies more on her team, work and business.

Her latest challenge is that she is avoiding having hard conversations with her team. As a result, people are getting away with things they shouldn't. When I walked into the business for the first time, I took one look around and said, "Let that person go." She said she would. Two weeks later, the person was still there. Deep down, my client is not okay with this person's poor performance, but she's also in the trap of wanting to be liked. On top of the guilt she feels over her unpredictable behavior, she's also trying to make up for a lack of social life by trying to create one at work. At her level, this is a clear conflict of interest.

We are just now starting to work on her self-awareness, and she is starting to build a social network outside of work so she can be the productive CEO she needs to be at work. Before she could start succeeding, we needed to first understand her feelings.

2. Leave your baggage at the door.

Prepare for the conversation you are about to have with your counter-party (who may, in the moment, act as your "combatant") and think ahead about how their words or actions will trigger you. Prepare to breathe deeply and reframe the conversation so you:

» Stay focused on a successful outcome

» Redirect their objections or passive aggressiveness into a productive way of thinking or action item

Through all of this, avoid injecting what stresses or bothers you into the conversation. This is not productive. Let the person on the receiving end air out their thoughts. Be a detective. Ask questions to pierce into the story they are telling themselves and the facts as they see them. Remember, team dynamics are incredibly subjective. You may have no idea about their context. The more you insert your feelings, the more you risk steering the conversation towards a mere reaction to issues you're raising rather than organic thoughts and experiences they are having. If you can solve the problem from where they are, you have won. Think of this phase as discovery. Don't muddle it with your own baggage.

3. Remind yourself of the weight of the burden, that you've been ignoring, being lifted

This is an esoteric concept. I get it. However, please try it. Rewarding yourself with positive feelings means making a long-term investment in yourself and your success. CEOs and leaders—we all dream big for our companies, but we don't dream big enough for ourselves. Prime your muscles to be rewarded for your efforts, and it will elevate your leadership and make it easier to have hard conversations. After all, the two go hand-in-hand, and you're not a martyr. You're a leader who is entitled to his/her own happiness.

Before having a hard conversation, think of the endorphin rush you'll feel at the end. It helps—trust me.

4. Understand the emotional state of the person you are addressing. Empathize with his/her potential reaction by placing yourself in their shoes.

This advice comes from a category of coaching called SQ, or social intelligence. Many people spend time planning for potential objections, and it is certainly a tried and true sales technique. Planning ahead for the emotional state of your counter-party takes this practice to the next level. This is because the range of potential objections will widen and evolve based on the emotional state of your counter-party.

We teach a 3-part technique for planning for hard conversations, which fits in perfectly with this step of EQ contextual mastery. The three parts are: 1) Pre-game, 2) Game and 3) Post-game. During pre-game (just like in sports), you plan and visualize. During the game, you play. You also leverage your mastery of this game by seeing plays as they happen and anticipating what comes next, as in chess. After it's done, you review what you've learned about yourself and your opponent, like athletes watching tape.

Let's put this in context with a real-life situation. If you're looking to challenge someone you know to be **passive aggressive**, plan accordingly. If you approach leadership thoughtfully, you would never treat this person the same way as someone who is direct, eager and an active listener. If you also know this person to be under an extra amount of stress and trying to meet deadlines, definitely take that into account as well. Context is everything, so in this case, delay the meeting, shorten the "stretch" you want them to make, be nicer on the first meeting to set up the longer play, etc.

A client of ours was struggling with a new executive they had hired. The executive wanted a specific title and was critical of the business in many ways. As a new member of the company, the owner was afraid to offend this person. What we learned was that this person appeared at first glance to be entitled and critical, but actually had never held a C-level title and was simply nervous. Despite his jitters, he was committed to his own growth, which we respected. We could have misunderstood his superficial behavior as cocky and entitled, but instead decided to ask the person questions to better understand their true motivation and their perspective in making this title request.

As a result of good communication and understanding, we decided to explain the gap in this person's experience, and how we were going to give him a chance to earn the title. We did not avoid the hard conversation of "this will be a stretch for you," but instead assumed he could reach the requirements of the title with the right guidance. We explained a way to get there, then allowed him to have the title and earn it at the same time. He was otherwise an A player. In our conversations, we asked enough questions to understand his motivation behind the title, his experience with other companies and titles and we added our perspective, which was admittedly different. Based on this well-laid foundation, he took one year to earn the lower end of the C-level title, and in the process, we inspired him, made him a participant in his own success and created more productivity than existed beforehand.

5. **Be ready to paint a picture of success to the person you are addressing.**

Keep your difficult conversations action-oriented and geared towards someplace positive. The reason for this is two-fold. First, it is always wise to be so aware of your counter-party's motivation and goals that you can align what you want with what they want. For example, if you want them to land a new client or hit a new sales target and they want a promotion or the opportunity to start traveling more on behalf of the company, voila—a clear path to making you both happy. Secondly, speaking to your counter-party within the framework of success puts you both in the mindset of winning, rather than self-doubt and potential disengagement when the conversation hits turbulence. It keeps things on track and stabilizes your mood, so you can stay motivated to get them where they want and need to go. Doubt breeds doubt, and positivity is just as contagious.

Execution Techniques to Make the Most out of Hard Conversations

On the execution side, to master hard conversations, you must first:

1. Define your vision

2. Know the trust level with your counter-party

3. Understand how far outside their truth you are pushing them

4. Divide the interactions into multiple stages

5. Speak persuasively and keep content relevant

1. **Define your vision**

It is important to define your intended outcome before starting a difficult conversation. You may even share it with your counter-party. This is really critical, because no matter how much you prepare, you will rarely anticipate all the twists and turns that hard conversations can take.

To understand your intended outcome, first ask yourself:

- » How do you want your counter-party to feel after the meeting?
- » What do you want them to believe?
- » What do you want them to achieve?

2. **Know the trust level with your counter-party**

Trust is an overused word and concept, so let's define it here for our purposes. When we talk about trust here, we are talking about understanding that intentions are coming from a good place—in both directions. We are not saying you need to trust everything your counter-party says or vice versa. Even people we "trust" are wrong in the way they execute things on occasion. This is why it's important for us to distinguish emotional trust from strategic or tactical alignment.

A **productive** amount of trust means:

1. Your counter-party will assume you have good intentions for them. Therefore, what you say will not trigger a defensive response.

2. They will hear your ideas, even if outside their comfort zone. Your ideas will be met with active curiosity as to how they

WILL work, rather than with skepticism as to how they won't.

An **unproductive** amount of trust means:

1. No matter what you say, your counter-party will assume the worst.

2. Your suggestions will be met with friction, and fall on deaf ears.

If you are **not** operating with a fair degree of mutual trust, it will be virtually impossible to turn hard conversations into productive outcomes with your intended party. If this is the case, and you have decided you want to invest in this person and help them become a valuable member of your team, you must first build trust with them before challenging their performance, skillset or personality.

3. Understand how far outside their truth you are pushing them
We all operate from our personal "truth." When we push people out of their comfort zone, we push them away from their current "truth." Knowing how far away someone is from the sought-after outcome helps you know the gap in skills they must conquer to achieve what you are asking. It is possible to move them closer to your goal, just take it one conversation at a time. You may also run into the objection that they are "too busy." This often means they are not prioritizing properly, so before you can work with them on achieving what you need, you must first help them learn to prioritize.

Once you've shared what you want someone to achieve, let him or her respond with ideas for solving the problem or getting there. If your team or team member engages and has ideas and is actively excited, they're not far at all from your "truth." If they're distant or say, "I don't know" and seem uninterested or put upon, you're making them feel that they are departing from their comfort zone.

4. Divide the interactions into multiple stages

If you're looking for something complex, and/or your counter-party is resistant, don't overwhelm them all at once. Walk them to the solution with multiple conversations, laying out bite-sized steps over time. If they're open to it and the problem is just complex, plan these steps and conversations together. This is a great way to get buy-in. If they're resistant, don't tell them in advance, and instead merely invite them to meet you again in a **short** timeframe. This tells the other person that you're committed to helping them, and that this whole endeavor is going somewhere productive. Put it off, and it'll feel unimportant, distant and hard to achieve. Movement at a pace is how things are accomplished, both at companies, and in life.

5. Speak persuasively and keep content relevant

Speak to win, not to be heard or loved. Too many of us have baggage, and we don't even realize when we are pushing others for boosts to our own egos. When we do this, we've lost sight of our intended outcome and are merely being bossy, or insecure, both of which are beneath us. Check your emotional needs at the door. Speak persuasively, and stay on topic. This will give your counter-party a fighting chance of processing your intended goals without getting lost in a swirl of irrelevant emotions.

QUICK TIPS FOR KEEPING PEOPLE ENGAGED:

1. Know your talking points and agenda before starting any meeting.

2. Know what you want people to feel and think after each meeting.

3. Ask questions to know where the people in the room are at emotionally and technically. Do they know what to do and how to do it? Are they ready to do what you need?

4. Keep your meeting(s) on time and on point.

5. Drive towards action. Seek tangible results.

6. Acknowledge everyone's involvement. Call out successful steps and mini-accomplishments as your team starts to achieve what you've asked them to do.

Chapter 3

Manage Your Energy Right

With a never-ending stream of tasks and a constant flow of information, the only way successful CEOs remain on top is by managing their energy.

Do you believe our personal energy is infinite? I do. Here's why. **Every time we want something badly enough, we achieve it.**

If you truly want something, envision it coming to life, allow yourself to be audacious in your ambitions, and then train your brain to withstand all doubt as you endeavor to achieve this goal. Easier said than done, right? Not with the right attitude towards **energy.**

8 EQ Steps Towards Transformative Energy Management

Here's how to manage your energy on every step of your journey towards successful leadership:

Before you start the journey:

1. Find your source

2. Know that thoughts create and either feed or starve your energy

3. Take stock of your beliefs

4. Wrangle your "inventory"

5. Understand that your potential is a concept towards which you must push yourself.

While you are on the journey:

1. Measure your energy level

2. Create a process for rebounding

3. Kill your energy vampires

1. Find your source.
I once believed I only had "so much energy." What a sad period in my life. It was simply not true. And no—age doesn't inform energy. The way I unlocked my energy potential was by way of experiment. I decided to check my calendar weekly for 3 months. I noted in my calendar energizing periods of time in green and non-energizing periods in red. At the time, I was 10% green, 90% red. Depressing, right? I was shocked, but after a while, I allowed myself to learn from it, and to change. I was tired at the end of every day, but that wasn't fair to my personal life. It wasn't easy, but I made myself start

to feel differently, and in time, I did. As I've said before, perception really is reality. I now have a framework for living: when I get home, I want to have **more** energy than when I left. It is amazing what I changed in my life to achieve this goal…and the fact that it was even possible. I changed my mindset about work. I discovered my love of service, and re-framed meetings from merely being CFO to teaching opportunities. My infinite energy comes from being in service. Where does yours come from?

2. **Know that thoughts create and either feed or starve your energy**

Take a quick test: visualize a sunny day, bright and full of warmth. Maybe you are out fly fishing in a beautiful gorge in Oregon with a friend, and you have a few cold beers in a rope sack in the cooler, flowing water at your feet and a ledge full of green grass and wildflowers where your tent is pitched with a fire pit and a picnic basket full of goodies. Feels good, eh? You're probably calm right now, and refreshed. Now, take part two: visualize the last piece of news you saw on TV. The last breaking news you can remember. That's it. Just do that, and let it sink in. Feels a little different, right? You're probably experiencing a small wave of anxiety, negativity, maybe even some depression. Enough said. Thoughts and contextual experiences either feed or starve our energy.

Our minds are the source of our fuel, but to operate at the highest level, we have to maintain a **high** quality of fuel in our tank. We have all kinds of thoughts that either enhance or pollute our fuel quality. As a result, when we turn on the engine, we either propel forward smoothly or lurch and grind forward at a pitiful pace.

3. Take Stock of Your Beliefs

I ask my clients to inventory their beliefs on a regular basis. What we think about is never in a silo. We're never just thinking about work, or our marriage. Thoughts intertwine, especially given the complexity of their context to each other. The older we get, the more they wrap around each other, like ever-deepening roots of a tree. That said, it is not impossible to untangle them for periodic emotional check-ins. When we do so, we're able to inventory our individual thoughts into three categories:

- » **Core Beliefs:** thoughts which serve both you AND your stakeholders
- » **Fear-Laden Thoughts:** thoughts that don't serve EITHER of those parties
- » **Gaps in Experience:** thoughts like "I don't know" are simply an indication that you have to gain new knowledge

4. Wrangle Your Inventory

Upon taking stock of your thoughts and current beliefs, take the following steps to root out anything unproductive:

- » Keep your core beliefs
- » Kill your fears
- » Learn through (and hence close) your gaps in experience

You'll find yourself gaining more and more momentum as you **kill fears** and **solve experience gaps**.

Do you believe the following?

If we try to focus our time and energy on our Core Beliefs, we empower ourselves to process all incoming information through our belief system. When we do this, we free ourselves from getting hung up on fears. We act. As Mihaly Csikszentmihalyi puts it, we "Flow."

QUICK TIPS FOR PROCESSING THOUGHTS:

- » When you're truly motivated to overcome your fears, you will do exactly that. You have to be ready.
- » As soon as you've conquered (or killed) your fears, start focusing on your vision. Every thought and action either moves you closer to your vision, or further from it. There are no "neutral" thoughts or actions.
- » Always be aware of your intentions.
- » Explore and reassess conflicting desires or fears.
- » If you act differently than your words, you will know you have not identified all of your fears.
- » Become a student of people. This is the lesson of a lifetime, and a class that thankfully never ends.

- » Master your positivity. Find your energy drivers. (Mine, as I said, are learning and service.)

- » Most importantly, have a vision—one that energizes you enough to carry you on every twist and turn of your path toward accomplishment.

5. Understand that potential is a concept towards which you must push yourself.

Potential. It is not tangible. It is not static. It moves, and evolves. There is no judgment in it, and no shame. Potential is an esoteric concept. Think of it as if you were a horse roaming a pasture. Consider the fence your potential. If you were to expand your fence, you'd have a larger space to roam, untethered by fear. Outside the fence are wolves and darkness. The practice of living life fully allows you to move your fences further and further out. Our potential is intrinsically connected to our mindset, our experiences, our networks and our mastery.

From wherever you are starting, start. Push your fence out. Test some boundaries. You might start small. You might just go for it. Either way, push. Have a friend listen to your life story. That will give them the context to give you some feedback—to let you know if you're being too conservative (i.e., staying safe inside your comfort zone) or too aggressive (living too far out of your comfort and skill zone all the time, thereby causing disruption and volatility wherever you go). Our words and stories are the keys to knowing our state of mind, and how far we can and should push ourselves.

"I am already successful. When I began working with Kothari Leadership, I was looking to increase sales. I know how my team and I grew our first $20 million. Through a combination of execution and emotional changes, I was able to take what I know, evolve it, and realize a whole new level of growth. My first step was emotionally accepting what got me here, and the fact that that wasn't all I needed to get to the next level. I had to catch myself from stopping my team and the Kothari Leadership team from thinking in new ways. New thinking is key. Those "new ways" were more strategic than I was used to in the past, and required patience and thinking. I was pushing for "now, now, now" and the "now" tactics had no leverage. Kothari Leadership helped me connect to an updated strategy, which led to my adding marketing talent and tactics to our success model. Now, my sales team has leads to work with, rather than always using their time to be lead generators and lead closers. I will admit that it was not easy to feel like I was slowing down. But in the end, we slowed down in order to speed up."

-**Brian,** *CEO of technology company*

6. Measure your energy level

Think of our energy in packets, rather than as a large mass. An easy method is a 1-10 scale. If you have a goal that you believe requires some level-8 energy because it is quite grand, then you will know the depth of the connection required between your vision and your inner drivers, and you will know you have to kill those fears that create friction in you swiftly so you can use your energy to focus on your goal. As you journey towards accomplishing your goal, you can check in with your current energy level, decide whether or not it's enough to sustain you as you push past your comfort zone, and recalibrate your thoughts, as needed. Take this model and duplicate it across multiple goals, over multiple years of your life in an ever-expanding array of great achievements, and you will find yourself the proud owner of a model of sustained success. When we remember, "it's all about the energy," we will always have a ledge to reach out to when our path takes an inevitable momentary dark turn.

"I was challenged by Kothari Leadership to clean up an old ownership relationship that was sucking money out of my company and energy from my life. My partner was no longer providing the value he once did. My comfort zone was avoidance. I was increasingly distracted to the point of being ineffective – so there was a cost to allowing this friction to continue. It took a lot of self-reflection and positioning, but I finally decided to have the hard talk(s). It was not one conversation with Kothari Leadership, but quite a few, as well as with my family. The whole time, I felt defensive. "Why is this all on me?" The truth was that it was my role to handle this problem, because I was the leader, good, bad and otherwise. I also experienced all the benefits of being the leader, and had to remind myself of that. Finally, I made it my "selfish" journey to learn how to have the courage to talk to my partner. I practiced how to be in a complicated unwinding of a partnership, as well as how to frame that negotiation to handle the complex emotions that would arise on both sides. Within five months, we were hammering out an agreement. It was complex and felt impossible at times, but with perseverance and the right skills and check-ins along the way, it got done! New comfort zone established! I had engaged in hard conversations. Negotiated a simple enough solution to a complex history. And now, I will forever be able to handle more complex negotiations as a result."

-**Dave**, *CEO of a healthcare company*

7. Create a process for rebounding

The further you are from your comfort zone, the less energy you will have to overcome all the objections life throws at you. As a result, the more you will want to quit. That is the very case for a healthier mindset. We all have times, maybe daily, when we feel we've lost our way, our energy, or both. This is a brain synapse, a knee-jerk reaction that our thoughts lapse into like a pothole on a weather-beaten road. To break free from it, we simply need a process for rebounding. Try this:

» **Call a friend in need.** For me personally, this triggers my true inner drivers—my passion for being in service…and my love of learning. I always learn something new when helping someone else.

» **Ask yourself what's causing your objections** – what fear is driving your current (albeit likely imagined) worst-case scenario? Understand that our minds create false scenarios. When they do, face these fears. Run at them, rather than from them.

» **Remind yourself what you're grateful for.** When I do this, my mood starts to lighten and my vision and goals fill me with a renewed sense of purpose. We all have things to be grateful for, if we choose to see them, and in thinking about them, we change our "state," as Tony Robbins says. According to Dr. Dan Radeicke, we also release endorphins when we feel gratitude, which—you guessed it—rebounds you back to a full tank of high quality (i.e., positively-motivated) fuel.

8. Kill your energy vampires

Whenever you are exhausted, remember you are reaching for your potential, and that takes guts. There are reasons to fail all around us. If we just keep our energy high, it will lift us past our challenges and elevate us to success. Identify your vampires, and then kill them. Vampires can be seen through the 9Lens framework™. Here's an example: if pointless meetings kill your energy, figure out a way to avoid them. There are answers to all problems. Never lose faith (which zaps your energy level). Instead, analyze what's challenging you, engage the people you trust for advice, and engage your inner resources to fix all problems.

Execution Techniques for Managing Your Energy

Here are some tried and true techniques for managing your energy:

1. Understand your role.
As high performers, we tend to have too many roles to play. It's important to assess each of your roles, and make sure they're all roles you want to keep. If there are roles you want or need to leave, prioritize doing so.

Worksheet: Inventory your Roles

Inventory your roles regularly, because we tend to take on more than we should. Don't forget one of your most important roles is taking care of yourself.

Role	Does it fit your life mission and business Core Purpose? (a)	Do the people/process/organization give you energy?	What needs to be changed for Column 3 to be "Yes" (b)
Example: Being the president of an entrepreneurial organization	Example: Yes, it promotes my learning to be a better leader. it is an organization that has a lot of learning opportunities. It will stretch my skills to lead other CEOs.	Yes, except some of the members.	My learning opportunity is to learn the gifts of the members I don't appreciate, align with that person to generate benefits to the organization of that person's gifts, and as a result, 1) my leadership will be better, 2) they will feel purposeful and 3) the organization will benefit.

2. Have a right-hand person.
Seems old school, but it's timeless, and in fact if you go back through history, you'll see this is a key part of how history gets made. Make sure you have a key "right-hand" person to handle your blocking and tackling. This is critical to preserving your energy.

3. Say no.
You'll need the energy to master the roles you do want to take on. Saying NO is harder than saying YES for most.

If you're at capacity, say no to new roles. If you know one of your current roles will expire soon, say not yet.

4. Manage your physical health.
This is so important. Whatever you do to stay healthy, stick to it. And if you're not healthy, make it a goal to get healthy. Mental energy only goes so far. It makes a world of difference having the physical energy to tackle your life's mission.

5. Book *you* time.
That's right. Put actual time on your calendar for yourself. Now, there's got to be a balance between serving yourself and over-indulging. This is tricky, but you ultimately know what you need to thrive. Invest in yourself, whether it's with a daily walk, yoga, or meditation. After these sessions, reflect back on your life's mission and core purpose. At least once a month, confirm whether you're still sticking to your framework. Make sure you're still on the right path to achieve your goals. If you're not, tweak what you're doing, and use your "you" time to evaluate and evolve.

Chapter 4

Conclusion

Successful CEOs don't happen overnight.

Amit's Story

In my twenties, I became the CFO of a public company, Autobytel. I felt I didn't deserve the role given to me by the very smart CEO and a board of prestigious overachievers. I had what has been coined, "Imposter's Syndrome." I felt like a fake. My twisted brain told me I wasn't worthy of the job, and as a result, I was always nervous. In reality, I helped triple the size of the company during my tenure, but every day was filled with anxiety and trepidation. I operated with one foot on the accelerator—constantly doing and achieving—and one foot on the brake, like a voice whispering, "You don't deserve this." In hindsight, I wonder what more I could have accomplished had I had a healthier outlook.

I remember a very specific day when the CEO pulled me aside. My first thought was, "This is it. I'm a fraud, and I've finally been found out." Instead, he said, "Amit, stop being so effing self-deprecating. You make me look bad for believing in you. You can do the job, so stop telling people you can't (through your overt and subtle word choices)."

That was a wake-up call, and it helped me reach a place where I was able to recognize my fears and run towards them—not away from them. Not only do I (to this day) see the benefits of this daily practice, but it's given my life more clarity and far more joy.

During my tenure at Autobytel, I realized I love people more than numbers. Once I had that revelation, I decided to do something about it. I hired my executive coach, Vance Caesar, to whom I owe everything in my career from that moment forward. He gave me the tools to rethink who I was and challenged me to perform at higher levels. Over the next few years, I went from CFO to COO. I finally had the courage to start my own business in an area I'm passionate about. As COO and CFO of Paciolan, Inc., I worked with a CEO of great talent and character. My philosophies thrived under his leadership. I was able to practice management philosophies that aligned perfectly with my beliefs, and time and time again, we exceeded the expectations of all of our stakeholders.

Now in having my own practice, I'm able to choose good people to be around, live with purpose, make a living, and spend time with my family. It didn't happen overnight. It took years, but I'm experiencing life in a way I never have before. I've finally figured out how to create the life I want. I have major responsibilities and still have major fears, but I'm now able to take them on and transform my challenges into my successes.

Over the last decade, I've been able to make sense of an efficient, yet simple way to organize my professional life. It's grown into the 9Lens framework™, which I hope helps you find your path to success and clarity as much as it's helped me and my clients find ours.

Conclusion

Thank you for reading Book 1 of The Kothari Method. I sincerely hope you find your framework helpful, and know how hard it is to put in the time and work necessary to set yourself up for transformative daily success. It certainly doesn't happen overnight, but definitely can make a profound difference.

If you're interested in delving deeper, Book 2 breaks down each of the 9 steps in far more detail. This is for CEOs ready for an intermediate-to-advanced approach to processing their ever-complex onslaught of information, data, goals and people.

Good luck getting rid of your chaos, facing your fears and prioritizing information so you and your team can achieve your vision. Put the hours in, and you'll wake up one day and realize you've created the exact personal and professional life you always dreamed of. Now, *that's* a good feeling.